For Lou,

The Book of Monsters

by

KEITH FLYNN

full of grace and light—
So nice to see you—

—Keith Flynn

ANIMAL
SOUNDS

Manufactured by Professional Press,
Jerry Cooper, PO Box 4371, Chapel Hill, NC.

Published by Animal Sounds,
PO Box 7086, Asheville, NC 28802.

ISBN 1-889276-01-4

Book design and typography by Lowell Allen,
62½ N. Lexington Avenue, Asheville, NC 28801.

Front cover painting:
"Man & Child," oil on canvas, 50" x 65", 1995,
by Donald O'Finn,
75 Flatbush Avenue, Brooklyn, NY.

Back cover photo taken by Stephen L. Wright,
Syracuse, NY, March 1995.

Grateful acknowledgement is made to the following publications
where many of these poems have previously appeared:
*The Asheville Poetry Review, Charlotte Poetry Review, Central New
York Environment, Fault Lines, The Fury, Lurch, The Manhattan
Mirror,* and *NC Arts and Entertainment.*

C O N T E N T S

LORD OF THE SMOKY MIRROR

for my Father

"No beast so fierce
  but knows some touch of pity,
  but I know none,
  and therefore am no beast."

Richard II
W. Shakespeare

Naming
The
Wilderness

THE RIGHT PLACE

He had come to this place
because he had been invited
and he had to be right,
everyone looked like him
and he had that longing
to be elsewhere
like he always did.
He started to ask someone
if this was the right place,
but they all said Shhh!
So he did.
When they sang, he sang too,
as they walked to the water
single file and drank together.
And when they laughed,
he laughed louder than anybody.
And when they wept,
he wept until they stopped.
When they let the man
mark their faces with chalk,
he stood in line
and pointed to his cheek.
He knew it was over
when they shook his hand
and everyone walked away,
back to the places
where they lived alone.
And he carefully took down
all the notes
from his refrigerator
and placed them in a box.
And he washed all the windows
of his house
and clipped his mustache,
because he'd made friends
and they might come.

GORGON

With two heads and three arms
and four eyes at civil war,
no wonder each advance
was confused as a personal affront.
Blasted from within by pure adrenaline,
how might the balance be reserved?
Each year piling cowardice upon appetite,
vanity retreating like a puddle in the sun.
No one to witness a handsome step
or plant a kiss upon that grinning snout,
discovery wasted, the sweet freedom of solitude lost,
while he pushed the rage of the world
back against it, the smoke from his nostrils
transforming each onlooker to stone.
The statues stand round silent and cold
and ignore the dying water that rattles
in their cracks that once was their blood.
The monkeys washing their dusty yams
in the stream do not look up
as the doomed one passes,
dragging his crowded shadow
like clothes a budding child
will soon outgrow.
The street suffers without horses,
without the memory of hooves on its back.
The crocodile without armor suffers,
naked to attack, naked as the grounded falcon,
forgotten in the ether of the sky.
Pity the poor Gorgon,
whose reflection is hideous to himself,
whose confusion is accompanied
by the roar of fate,
whose madness is circled
by the clatter of mirrors.
Who witness to his own descent
sees in each natural act only treason,
wandering alien in the museum of identity,
brother to nothing in this world.

APOSTROPHES

"the pure products of America go crazy..."
To Elsie, 1923
—William Carlos Williams

My friend Harry is a Brooklyn attorney
who just fell out of love.
We sit at his fourth floor apartment
looking out the window,
while I listen to him lose his religion,
denounce his woman and his life.
The Cammareri Bros. Bakery
mixes its smell
with the Henry Street Fish Market.
In the harbor, the lights
from the Statue of Liberty
flicker off and on at Europe
like red rhinestones.
Lyle Lovett is singing,
"get back chip-kicker, redneck woman..."
Disenfranchised Pontiacs
crawl from alley to alley
looking for a warm place to hide.
"She ain't no lady," Lyle sings,
"she's my wife."

We have to stay connected, Harry says,
and I agree,
we have to stay connected,
to a will, a person, a focus, a feeling.
When all about us disengages,
when the streetlights fail
and blink out, steaming in protest,
we have to stay
and stay
connected.

I'm 34, she said,
Sunday evening in a Tupelo blues bar,
chattering about the Gulf war on cable,
like watching the latest episode of Dynasty.
Women must say this to you
all the time, she says.
You're one handsome man.
I have two small children
and I don't get out much.
You're driving me crazy.
A guy walks by in a black T-shirt,
NUMBSKULL emblazoned on his chest.
He couldn't slow down fast enough.

There ain't no sunshine, she says.
I can't live like this forever.
I could do almost, well you know, anything.
A good woman drew my husband away.
I knew her, she used to come down here
and watch him play.

He played harp, blew so hard
it sounded like a freight train.
Honor the dead, she says,
waving her hand,
honor the dead and let 'em rest.
Musicians are just shit anyway,
vain & powerful, all I seem to get.

Elvis lives near here, she says.
He does.
Close to the house his Daddy built
for a hundred and eighty bucks.
Borrowed it from somebody or other.
Yeah, everybody knows Elvis 'round here.
He wouldn't just leave us hanging.
We made him, you know, simple folks,
and he wouldn't do nothing to hurt that.

'Round midnight,
somewhere in the South,
Thelonious Monk is playing piano,
Trinkle Tinkle,
and some idiot comes
out of the crowd playing banjo,
but he is in tune,
on the one
and Monk stays calm,
keeps his head down,
sweaty concentration
dripping on his hands.

Bill Monroe comes walking
out of the ladies room
zipping his fly,
"She blew me so hard," he says,
"I went straight to the top
of the country charts,
and almost crossed over into pop!"

The Wolf is coughing in a dark corner,
"I asked the girl for water
and she gave me gasoline!"
His kidneys dried out like two fat plums,
he hacks an evil sound
into the mike and roars,
eyes bulging.
The lights linger and roll off.

"Too primal for ordinary folks," they say,
"way too much."
They paint the biography
of a naked ape
and shake another acrobat from his wire.

Agony is what they pay to see,
martyrs of the imagination.
Poor Monk floated in and out
of sanitariums until the end
when he could no longer
recognize his son.
He stopped playing,
opened the lid on his piano stool
and stepped in,
dropping out of sight.

These shadows that squirm
about my heart's garden
are my brothers,
and they cling like parasites
to the furry underbelly of America,
the mongrel that kills
what it cannot unravel,
or forgets what it cannot trap
in the ferocious Coliseums
where enormity dwindles
to a single signal, a gunshot,
a laughing light
that winks on when it is happy
and winks off when it is not.

4–91
Memphis

THE EMPIRE OF THE SPIDERS

With a baseball bat,
I slashed and shattered
the empire of the spiders,
whose silver chains
had conspired with the sun
to hem me in my own house.
At night they waited anxiously
until the snoring confirmed my sleep.
Then they began.
Between the blades of jagged grass,
they stockpiled little softballs of dew
and tore ropes from the water.
Out of their bellies,
an endless string unraveled,
formed a catwalk
and a moist shaky tapestry.
They sat in the center
of their cathedrals & shivered
until the light held.
The sun loved them,
flooded their castles
with worship and with prey.
The spiders feasted,
ignoring my heavy bat
as their cities grew
more and more elaborate.
The routine became ritual
until finally the sun refused even me.
My wife swallowed a spider
and it exploded inside her,
leaving a silken mummy
that I could not love.
She stumbled through the field at night,
plunging the points of her breasts
into the moon.
What was I to do?
I waged a final assault
and watched the juices splatter
before the webs tightened in fists
around my bat. I surrendered,
locked the door and left,
pausing for a second as the sun rose
and the yard came alive, alive with spiders
looking for somewhere soft to land,
somewhere solid to build again.

RODEO CLOWN

Laughter booms from old cowhands
fast chicken feet
confusing the bull again
Red mop hair flops
bowing to the crowd
while delighted children dance
sucking cotton candy
down
down
the lights fall dying
and after the clouds
of dust have settled
after the pricked ribs
of the horses have cooled
after the face paint
smears the porcelain
and slithers down the drain
The dark comedian
remembers himself
the grime a grain
of water cannot touch
the true color of his hair
the fierce ache curled
in every joint
the steady dragon stare

BELLEYE

Melvin ambled through forgotten streets
whose names owed their life to arithmetic,
where a man could pass his hours
shifting his bones, beating a dead rhyme,
1st street, 2nd, and so on, the family circle
that wears down concrete parallels.
Melvin's estate was Chaplinesque,
a beaten derby and a faded vest,
an old gold chain that had no watch
and a pocket for his knife.
He had one eye that was larger than the other,
set at an angle like a bell about to ring.
Watery and soft, it served as a compass
moving Melvin from side to side, as if his feet
had forgotten their purpose and just followed the eye,
like a flounder's blunt body trailing a murky ocean light.

I attended elementary school on an island,
in the middle of a river, a half-mile
from Melvin's domain on the courthouse steps,
where the town's one yellow streetlight
winked caution, caution, slowing the occasional
echo of a car. I was twelve then, my friends thirteen,
and we left school promptly at the stroke of three,
bursting with untapped energy, bored and mean,
blowing across the bridge into town.
We had two hours to kill before practice,
baseball or basketball, there was no difference,
the seasons dictated the way our feet would run.
Melvin was our special prey, and we were
delighted as we watched him squirm.
"Belleye," we shouted as we had heard before,
like the older boys who had opened the door
and released the torrent of ridicule
that we poured on Melvin.

> "Belleye," we yelled and yelled some more
> as the little man wheezed and broke into a trot,
> fishing in his pocket for the knife.
> He brandished his little dagger and screamed
> high-pitched syllables that never formed words.
> We believed he couldn't speak, but were never
> sure, there was too much foam in his rage
> and it washed out the meaning, breaking
> against the stone cliffs of our faces.
> Melvin never caught us, but he tried.
> He lurched about like an animal in pain,
> stabbing the air with his knife.

We ran and shrieked until the town clock
bonged five, then we scampered back
into respectability, back into the uniforms
with our names on the shoulders,
that the town fathers had bought
for us a century ago.

        Melvin we left behind with his own ghosts.

I never thought of this until I returned home
sixteen years later and read Melvin's obituary
in the local rag, sitting on the courthouse steps
I had desecrated as a child. Melvin had gone in his sleep,
lying on the warm railroad tracks, never hearing
the horn or seeing the engine's single yellow eye
bearing down on the spot he had made his bed.

They knew it was Melvin
                  because the dented derby
        lay testifying in the grass.

I stood on the bridge and looked down the tracks,
watched the river meander under my feet and around
the island where the condemned school building
stood empty and beaten, its clay roof burned pale
by the sun. Framed by this scene, I remembered
the old streetsweeper with no teeth who told me
how Melvin had acquired his name.

It seems Melvin had know some fame in his youth.
In his twenties he had chopped up his wife with an axe,
mailed her various body parts around the country
and cut out his own tongue so he wouldn't confess.
At his trial he passed a tablet to the judge
with a twofold message. On the one hand, pleading insanity,
and on the other, asking permission to serve
as his own defense. With some success he was denied
the latter and awarded the former by a jury of his peers.
Belli the Great, they called him, after the noted attorney,
and he served out his sentence in the asylum shuffling
through the halls for twenty years. Upon his release,
he found his way back to Marshall, the town of his birth
and served as a reminder to the dark skull leering behind
each rosy face. Belli the Great, a mumbling mediator
with wild hands, harmlessly negotiating the disputes
between garbage cans, wandering the streets as if in
a trance, unrattled in his favorite dream, riding
a railroad car, trusty blade in his fist, lying in ambush
behind a pack of boys, certain to silence the fated name
if he, quickly enough, could lay his hands on just one.

THE TEMPORAL PLAIN

The cowboys of LSD have re-surfaced,
galloping across the temporal plain,
peddling faster and faster
until their minds open out
like an Arizona sky.
One by one they leap
into their video screens
and crawl like ants
through the keyhole of virtual reality.
Disembodied information
holds them weightless in Ritual World,
seized by consensual hallucinations.
They swim forward seeking cybersex,
the perfect experience,
the sugar cube of truth,
peering like voyeurs
through the microscope lens
at naked gods that couple & divide
in an ocean the size of a teacup.
Erotic identities fall away,
and suddenly,
the prison of Socrates is made plain,
frozen like Van Gogh, a scab
painting to heal himself,
desperate to learn Christ's simple passion,
the love without decor,
the Beauty that beat at his sill
until the lights blew out,
and forced him to decorate with insanity
colors beyond human understanding,
as he stumbled drunken, hysterical & sweet
toward ultimate reality,
the bright rainbow landscapes of the damned.

THE GARDEN OF EARTHLY DELIGHT

Everything sags here,
sluggish animal laughter,
cigar smoke clinging to the deli door
like a black diaper,
meat-filled intestines
that grow thin and push
an icy pain through the body
like a dorsal fin carving miles
of boundary between the estranged lungs.

The store clerk says please
when he means perfectly fine
or perhaps or even pardon me.
His please drips like a faucet
and resonates with obscenities.
He motions in the doorway
for someone to come inside
and he can't decide if he
should embrace or deride the patron's
heavy pondering over the price
of the creamy peanut butter
as opposed to the chunky
with real peanut bits.

Too many grams of fat, they surmise,
and he swells with impatience,
but says nothing,
certain he will be rewarded
for this levity of spirit.
He stammers & then thinks better of it,
wizard of weary silence.
Drooping through the store
like an octopus, his jelly face
drifts from anger to beatitude
in a blue-green funk
of shelves and shifting fortunes.

His favorite singing dancing
yoga girl bops down the aisle.
She laps up the dried dates
for breakfast & quiets the knives,
telling him, "God is my instrument,
there is no such place as far away."
In a month she is gone to live
with her mad narcoleptic mother
who hisses in her sleep
like a mongoose battling poisonous vipers.
Postcards come from Colorado
with no return address,
only rocky cliffs burned savage red
and topped with a scoop of snow.

The dull days double in bulk.
A cumbersome lava-colored Buddha
waves hello in the front window,
ignoring the whistles & shrieks of traffic,
drizzling motors braked to a growl.
They leak a black film
that smothers the sidewalk,
so the clerk terrorizes the taxis
with his water hose and aims
graceful arcs in the direction
of a skinny sinking Puerto Rican man
teetering on the curb.
He mumbles to himself in Spanish
and patiently crumples
bits of paper, popcorn-size,
feeding his slender poems to the birds.

MOUNTAIN MAN

We stop in a small beat town
in Tennessee, hungry for pizza.
The plaque on the wall reads,
Barry's Tricopherus,
the oldest and the best,
guaranteed to restore
the hair to bald heads.
As soon as we are seated,
an evil spirit
invades the jukebox,
playing some vanilla country
and hanging the record,
the record,
the record.
The country Cleaver
across the room can't take it.
He deserts his loud happy clan
and slams the box off the floor
three times before it relents.
There, he says.
I watch his woman
and I know,
he is the one
her mother warned her about,
a take-charge,
a rah-rah,
a mountain man.

THE HOUSE OF NIGHT

From the progeny of chaos
to the comfort of strangers,
how deep can I go?
Faced down by the ferocious longing
of a creative universe,
what do we teach the little ones?
When the death camp survives,
turning back the blue angel,
what reckless definition will cool
the evening glare, the whistling river's
grand claustrophobia?

Diaper Dan, Vice-Robin
to the Presidential Batman,
perks up when pointed toward Sarajevo.
Alas Boy Wonder, look askance, no oil there.
A noxious election vapor bubbles up,
shadowed by Vietnam, ethnic cleansing,
collateral damage, matchstick jubilees
defending fraternity & the status quo.
Los Angeles smolders, the oil fields
of Persia are an oasis,
wheels within wheels of suffering,
candle derricks burning on
a deserted birthday cake.

Somalia is too weak
to bury her dead,
powerless between two worlds,
stripped from the casement,
her scorched regal dignity
pregnant with the best intentions,
raving as she falls in fitful
disbelief from the precipice.

Imagine the Golden Gate Bridge
toppled by the weight of human beings.
Imagine the seventh son
of a third generation Congressman
awake for the first time,
accustomed to winning,
spoonfed promises on Rodeo Drive
between the bananas & champagne,
screaming, what vague crucifixion is this?

Imagine a child with his legs flying,
impaled on the horn of a rhinoceros.
Imagine Bangladesh
when the typhoon hit
and terrified parents
tied their babies to trees
to keep them from being washed away.

For twelve months, besieged by these visions,
I have dreamt of children
like milk-white peacocks
unfolding from their trees,
their rainbow fans bobbing
beneath a crimson sky,
their lost cities surfacing one by one,
islands of roses rising in their eyes.

America is a great spirit bird
caught in the house of night,
ramming home alternative slogans
behind telephone lines,
between the darkness of her windows.
1-900- FUCK ME, SUCK ME, BEG ME, SHRED ME,
wrap me in yellow ribbon & watch me go
straight to the Pennsylvania state border,
running parallel to the Mason Dixon Line.

The Great White Way starts here,
above Mauzy Broadway's endless caverns,
beneath the Big Apple's urban blight,
right on the American Legion Memorial Highway,
23 miles to the Gettysburg Address,
four score and seven years
from the shores of Tripoli.
Kentucky Fried McComfort Inns
as far as the eye can see.

> August 13–16, 1992
> on the eve of the GOP convention

THE UNFRIENDLY CHILD

The unfriendly child
that haunts Mother Russia
sees through a crack
in the wall,
Rabelaisian satellites,
poetry glowing
like velvet uranium
on the pages
of dangerous books.
A dark neighbor
stares back,
cursing the water
that covers his gate
in a bedlam
of rainbows.

The daughters
of limestone,
stripped from their mother,
are being auctioned
like onions.

Coffin ships splinter
in the bay,
betraying the land
& its many hungers,
some supernatural need
to corner all the seeds,
all the vines of grief
in the world
and barter nothing,
distribute across
the puzzle
of these wild idle acres
only fog & mourning,
a famine of memories
flying off like steam
into space.

THE ROAD FROM GUATEMALA

Rebels in the low hills,
hungry for home,
hugging the great rocks of their youth,
watch the tourists
wriggle two to a phone booth,
biting beads,
trying on hats and handcrafted spoons,
in pursuit of the perfect chili dog.

Vines rise over these skinny trees,
dank canals, buckshot abandoned cars.
The brown rivers ooze silently
through the jungle
with their smell of shit & unwashed hair.
Crowds of flowers sway there
on the bank, basking in lavender,

brought to bloom by waste,
or wasted, like the roads
that curl in questions from the city,
whose stones falter poised to drop,
but do not know where.
Like a blind man's tattered boots,
they wait, suspended in confusion,
frozen at the bottom of the stairs.

INDIAN SUMMER

The Indian Summer
lingers
like a coda,
an uneasy stranger
wrapped
in the surreal
colors of
dying trees.

Open holes
suck
the chilled air
down,
while
the remote sun
descends
like
a drop of blood.

An arrowhead
of strange geese
floats
along
the storm's
ominous edge,
unafraid
of failure.

They know
if dreams
curve
into being
for no reason,
there would
linger
a trail
in the memory,

an O
at the
quiet center,
where
the storm's
invisible
pin
stays warm.

THE PLEASURE WHEEL

You see,
    my swollen ankle
points my useless foot
    toward the rising sun.
                My hip points west.
  I hop, slide, hop, slide, sideways
        through the gaping crowd.
Like a bird with its beak
        on the side of its head,
    I hammer against the wind.
Like a gnarled branch twisted by the weather,
    I grow in stops
        and starts,
   disregarding the violent energy
    invading my limbs,
   the hungry winter that sucks
       my movement away.
My withered foot is fitted
          with a special shoe,
a platform heel I can ride.
When the a cappella groups on the corner
step aside for the brothers & their boxes,
    full of watery music,
I climb up
    on my crooked foot and swing
  like a revolving door.
          I pivot
  like a walnut on its edge.
I throw out my arms above the fuzzy pavement
        and shake
like a last maple leaf on its weakening stem,
spinning in the center of the black boys
      with their beaten smiles.
Ballerina, they yell, ballerina,
  before they fall
     down
      laughing.
I turn and turn,
before my poor hip protests and I stop,
    hop, slide away.
Satisfied and shining like mica,
           I tumble
complete into the stew of eyes.

WAFER

If the moon fell on you
one thick night
when you were walking along,
afraid that gargoyles were awake,
and you picked up that moon
and took a bite,
it would stick to the roof
of your mouth like peppermint.

And you wouldn't worry
about gargoyles flying
over the countryside.
And it wouldn't matter
if you caught them
smirking in the dark
when you turned your head.

No, you would forget
and wonder,
how could this moon
come apart like candy
on my tongue
and still hold so much light?

The Hybrid Principle

GERONIMO

Nine days in a row
at a hundred degrees,
tomato vines limp as confetti.
The bridges all seem higher.
Planks are missing,
and the people, in love's slipstream,
chant winter tantras
behind their misty faces.
The thin creek begins to bare its bones,
the creek where we cornered
dozens of crayfish
and forced them to fight to the death
in a plastic wading pool.
Fifteen years ago,
one champion lasted the summer.
We named him Geronimo,
because his claws churned the water
in every direction,
and he understood the attack,
how pandemonium in the skull
of the underdog was to be expected,
how each sound piles upon the other
and must be stripped away.
When my silhouette grew
and whispered the first strings
of beard on my face,
a tide deep in my body
remembered Geronimo,
remembered the way the rock and root
held the hill in place.
Before all this erosion.
Before I found the mirror's loneliness,
and projected my good standing
by the way I shaved my face.
Before I learned to toast to Satan,
and sent my spirit sprawling,
amazed and defiant,
undressing as I dropped
cleanly into manhood.

IN ANOTHER LIFE

In another life, nimble as a puppeteer,
with nothing left to dig for,
she might have pulled the floss
through her teeth more quickly, she said,
satisfied that the source of her discomfort
was hidden in a storm,
a bur that had been with her forever,
snatched up and thrown back,
like an island buried beneath the sea.

Her husband released it
when he stabbed her fourteen times,
because an anonymous caller
set the canyons of his mind ablaze.
She lived to drop the charges, she said,
because he too was afraid,
but her body is dotted with stars,
windows where the dull glow
of another life show through.

INSIDE THE WHITE HORSE

Inside the White Horse
where Dylan Thomas
began to dislocate his senses.
June 22, with whiskey lens
I see through the bottom of my glass
        outside,
          excited silhouettes
          fighting back,
peeling away their garments of distress.
Bones swell under togas,
and in every bulging heart, said Rimbaud,
there beats the double sex.

A murderer stalks gay men in Milwaukee.
Herman Angel raises a toast.
He just floated from Harlem to Amsterdam
seeking cannabis for his pipe.
He's a Latin piano player
        who knows Sonny Rollins
        and his quintet needs a name.
        He suggests Superman's Disease
        and submits it for our approval,
says his dick is a Chinese brush,
        a scented aphrodisiac.
He drinks strictly vodka.

Beatrice lands down
beside him, just cooling, she says.
Beatrice is recovering.
Her parents were Harvard '53
        and Yale '54,
            respectively,
archaeologist
and author
        seeking world exotica.
Once in Rio,
        they observed The Candomble
        with eight year old Beatrice in tow.
The small blonde child began to hum
        with the atabaques,
            and became distraught,
        her movements automatic
        as if she was swimming in thin air.

Nervous evil jerks
tittered through her limbs
as she grazed the dark horn.
Her parents, frightened,
                    covered her
            with veils & she vomited,
            bruised like a mango,
            her thin skin smoky.
Twenty-five years later,
sometimes she forgets where she was
                    a moment before,
her hands clammy and her eyes burning.

Herman Angel says he has a friend
whose father was mauled by a bear
in Yellowstone Park.
                    He says
the man lost his fearful equilibrium
and believed he was St. George,
            radiant as a laser,
                    ready to spear the dragon
for the lion-hearted greater good.

His son grew like a geyser into manhood,
killing everything he could find on Safari,
            tigers, lions, elephants,
                    and hangs
                    their heads
on the wall above the urn
where his father's ashes rustle.

Any man who has felt a man inside him
or tasted a boy
in his mouth,
                    romps defiantly
                    down Hudson St. today,
parading in masks
with the burlesque of Oxala,
                    fangs
                    gleaming,
while mute fires stretch and ripple
behind the buckled doorways,
                            intently listening
    as the regiments
                    scatter out
                    in crowns of roses.

A burly blue hatred
     is swirling
     like a thief
          in the windows
and around
         the maple hearth
         of the White Horse,
chilled mugs click in agreement,
      tongues wag in measured tones.
Pee Wee Herman is arrested for jacking off.
The white terrace sweats.
          Chaos
          reigns
          in the flowerpots.

THE JAMES RIVER EXPRESS

It was something he said to her
when they stepped off the platform
and into the James River bus,
something sharp, but stated
in a low voice, something
only a stranger would understand.

The cities retreated on both sides.
The wine swam round in their bottle
as her fingers crawled up his leg,
through his hair, on his chin.

The windows looked down
and held them swimming,
their fierce instincts strutting
like weasels, but their faces
and skin were silent,
their bodies barely moved.

Patience hung between them
like a wreath,
like an early morning wind
that blows its soft tempo
from room to room.

Her mother told her,
all men are dogs, watch them
and she did, she watched him sleeping,
watched one hair curl like a comma
on his cheek.

Then she knew her mother's horror
and felt fear enough to kiss him,
to whisper softly in his mouth,
Giselle, Giselle, her name.

UNDER A HUNTER'S MOON

When Aktaeon waded into the forest,
he was blood-ready,
pampered hounds on both sides
scouring the brush for game.
What they found was Diana,
turning in a quiet lake,
making hoops in the water
with her hands.

Startled, her soul rolled beneath her
in a thousand shapes,
hatred in her eyes.
The hounds circled smiling,
and the hunter stumbled,
helpless and surprised,
dizzy with the grief of his new fur,
knowledge at his throat like a knife.

THE MEN'S MOVEMENT

I was thinking of Chicago
and wind and Little Milton,
how he hated the icy gusts
that roared thru the boards
from Lake Michigan so much
that he sang in a whisper of protest,
a buttery vibrato
that hardened into stories
and held the wind's woman
hostage inside them.

I am twenty-nine years old today,
jogging with my friend when two boys
whip past us on silver bikes,
the one leaning toward the other & saying,
"I don't go too fast down this hill."
I have never been to Chicago
and I didn't go to my class reunion
and every hill is an Everest
because I'm not a boy anymore
and besides, all my classmates
came to see me and my band
and said how strange I looked
with all my hair and sideburns
and howling and almost thirty
and what did I do with myself anyway?

Well, I'm a man, I answer,
or as Robert Bly would hasten to add,
"a mythopoetic Iron Man on a spiritual odyssey."
When I think about being a man
I stand in the corner and flex my muscles
like Arnold the Barbarian,
the ultimate immigrant success story,
a gene pool of pathos & testosterone,
a Republican with the juice
to seduce a Kennedy.

For the first time I believe
my body is against me,
or as Frost said, "I think
how little good my health
did anyone near me."
There are spies inside my skin,
nocturnal emissions,
winds that hammer through my joints
and whisper on the peaks of my shoulders
that he can't tell his right hand
from his left.

This is what we are taught.
Be strong. Head a Family.
Hide well your Faults.
The last is easy.
We learn to negotiate our silence early,
herding like cattle
around a block of salt.
We are a sleepy regiment in retreat,
goaded with New Age jargon,
thrashing through the forest
with our huge heads in our hands,
like children stealing melons,
stiff with monstrous thoughts.

OZONE PARK

In the scratched sky
a plane is pasted
on a zig zag pattern,
dragging a banner that says,
PLEASE MARRY ME.

A woman stands up on her balcony,
her breasts bare and shimmering.
Sweaty and disoriented from the sun,
she watches the plane
for a second, mesmerized,
as if the message were a personal one,
someone sure of success
asking her to marry and marry
and make us something.
She steps out of her panties
and walks inside,
cool carpet against her feet.

A man stands in the street
shouting at a building
that never answers.
Hurry and be done with it, he says.
On his car radio,
a cornerback feels the receiver
see the ball and lowers his helmet
like a boulder.
He feels the back tense & go down
into a cauldron of numbers.
Stamping and snorting, the bodies
pull him in and the crowd explodes.

The spittle of a hydrant
loops up & around the tingling limbs
of three black children
who have captured a jellyfish
in a blue bucket.
It shivers like a tiny pink ocean,
a sliver of living marmalade.
They look up in unison at the plane,
purring toward home, its stark plea unheeded.

The man receives his answer,
and the woman, showered and powdered,
dressing for dinner,
watches the children on the pier.
She shrugs & turns away as the sun gives up,
while they sing and prance
and flip a stiff jellyfish
headfirst into the shriveling waves.

WHILE I WAS AWAY

What I fought to win, I give back.
I will let the tributary of my flesh
roll silently through the ravines
and underground springs,
the solemn rooms naming no one,
whispering nothing.
Until your breasts soften with peace.
Until the hollows of your hips
ring with the hidden violins
murmuring in every tree.
Until your wells shine with me,
reverberating my quiet name,
making our hushed story repentant,
the color of quartz.
Shattered and frozen,
the white hills are humming under snow.

THE BEES OF LEISURE

The hive is antiseptic,
        a cortisone chamber
    of vicious cycles
where all burn for love.
        The queen's pinprick
is interrupted
      by the penetration
of a dozen scouts.
Canyons unwind in her living room.
    Meat-eating birds,
        with out-stretched wings,
    perch on the Lazy Susan.

Sinless and somber,
        suckled on honeycomb,
    the bees of leisure
hover buzzing by the pool,
        having come fashionably
    in their own due time,
nibbling melon and caramel,
      masturbating
          conversation.

Lunacy and sexual detectives
        smother the hive,
      poisoning the larvae
    for their own good.
The queen bristles
      like a porcupine,
    but says nothing,
        each orifice
    stuffed
with designer candy canes.

The Aquarian Brigade,
        fresh from
      a Woodstock Reunion,
    paddles away in the last canoe.

THE CEMETERY ON MASHBURN HILL

I

The stations have signed off,
flushing their static
into every channel
and I cannot sleep.
I follow my feet
into the amber twilight
along the cowpath
toward the river.

The tombstones here are so old
that many have crumbled
or broken in two.
A piece of a forgotten name
is slowly crawling beneath the moss.
Pockmarks in these plaques
hold bellybuttons of evening dew,
a thousand thimbles
of one-celled organisms
tuned to the rush of the river.

The beaded green lilies turn
like rhinestones, clinging
to the fragile bank.
A mist obscures the trees,
changing its shape as it hovers,
hugging the water
like confused angels
struggling to fly upstream.

The angels are everywhere,
landing for a moment on the water,
slithering like fog
through the cracks in these stones,
foaming from the distant chimneys.

II

My father's failing head
rests across the river like a turnip.
You got to be something, he told me,
when I was fourteen, afraid to wake him,
carefully petting my first lover
on the couch as her eyes filled with fear.

A rabbit nibbling a grave
hops in parabolas with the sky.
The moon drips down
like a golden tear
gaffed in mid-flight.

I remember how we squirmed
and rested and cried
like these crickets in the trees,
swollen from singing,
clinging to the leaves for dear life.

A newborn's tiny monument
is the only solid marker on the grounds.
I step lightly past the little plot
and imagine in the fog,
a woman walking toward me
holding a child in her arms,
her breasts draped in noodles of moonlight.

III

Earlier today, my mother stood peering
in the mirror, posing an out-dated red bikini,
her arms stretched toward the ceiling
in a halo, her heavy breasts
jammed together by a top too small,
saying over and over,
my ribs have disappeared.

Locked in her body like a pebble,
shiny as a skate, I began to slide.
Furs and shadows trembled
as I broke into light,
a bundle of stars the size of a ball,
chained to her, biting and tugging
at the body that would betray us both,
stretch between us time and again
like the dark webbing of a dream,

as time itself hardened
to support our mistakes,
to record our recoveries,
to lift us upon the steeple of old age
in a whirlwind of love.

So dark are the stations of desire.
A single thread of silver
has sunken a falcon miles below,
while the frogs bellow in mock celebration.
Their cruelty is deafening,
gorgeous and precise as the moon
moving on like a cruise ship
in the vapor, heavy with angels.

AMERICAN TRAGEDY

O Guyana, does the ghost
of Jim Jones,
pulsing with epiphanies,
wander your jungles
and cry to the quilted birds?
Morbid self-absorption,
the world grows as weary
of us as we do of it.
And no one goes crazy alone.
We need accomplices,
keen to learn our weakness,
anxious to tell us
how the dumb earth
ticks to a halt.

American tragedies
are that deliberate,
built solidly with small
increments of rebellion,
constructed a drop at a time,
like the boy enduring
the promises
and pennywhistle hymns
of a ancient church,
throwing his knife
at the back of a pew,
spitting in his hands,
like his father did,
every time it sticks.

THE KITES

Back and forth the boats roll,
light as chiffon, their one sail
drooping like a broken wing.
Time is not a constant spillway
of rare and imagined windows,
pulsing with light catastrophes.
Its pictures have many dimensions
that crinkle and crouch,
witnessed invisibly by bodies
born bruised into light,
whose movements we cannot amend.

These children on the beach
jerk under kites,
running against their clothes,
brimming with a wonder
they cannot keep.
With many tongues they ripple silently,
prey to the whims of melancholy mountains,
or smiling humped assassins,
the seaweed phenomena of the past
that chokes to a standstill
the calm pools that govern its life.

The rain in the trees
is slowly walking away
like a giant woman
streaming silver flowers
upon the air,
climbing higher & higher
into the unruffled sky,
tiny kites tangled in her hair.

THE HYBRID PRINCIPLE

We have met before.
When the puddles
were silent as mines.
When we were a single color
blasting from the mouth
of a brass clarinet.
I knew you would recognize me.
Even as I am unable to recall your name.
But I recall the tightrope
of your smile,
those lips that hovered over me
like dragonflies,
lapping the shadows from my skin.
And your eyes,
stronger than the elves of Self,
swallowed my image & watched it grow.
I have never seen me so clearly before.
That evening, the wind was so light
that it pushed the night
like pudding
through the trees.
The shingle of your scent
was matted in the charcoal of my hair,
and everywhere, the metal echoes of death
were drowned in the sweetness.
The cries and blasts
of the battered horizon
gripped together
to form an architecture of neglect.
We painted over it,
painted over the suffering graffiti,
painted over the generals & their chimneys,
dressed in soot.
We called the suicides
from their bridges
and welcomed their amnesia
and our color covered everything,
everything we had seen,
red yellow blue white green.

Lord
of
The
Smoky
Mirror

STARFISH

Furry
mounted by light

a myriad desert silence
is carried by your little jets

You are the nucleus of prayer
drifting like faith

layer upon layer
toward a God you cannot see

A prop twirling in the blue heaven
pulls your delicate hand

waving slowly adieu

You are a flower
circling in the foamy orchard

In the calm expanse
you tinkle like a shy comet

you sigh
inside
the reef

IMAGO

The cicadas are awake.
Every 17 years they come
humming from their holes,
a vast Om shivering in the air,
beating their four parts
blindly in the fresh light.

The adults mate and die.
The children sink underground
and wait, then come groaning up
like infallible pantomimes,
every 17 years, breeding hallucinations,
a herd of purring, dreaming locusts.

In her garden an old woman stoops,
unbothered by the constant drone
of singing insects, ignoring the caterpillar
and its ever-changing wrinkle,
the potato whispering to the woodchuck,

hide and watch,
regard the wind
and its ancient wings,
the swallow, the thrush
the black laughing critic, the crow.

The old gardener moves from leaf to leaf,
gripping a weathered sunflower
between her fingers, cradles its head
in the palm of her hand and peels it,
feels with much delight

the weathered petals go limp,
and discovers her own haggard likeness
staring back, its leather head unblinking,
clenched like a fist
against the sky.

JUMP SHOT

Now I understand
the voices that rustled
in the forest
calling my name.
Why I sloshed
in a muddy field,
snow or rain,
balancing a leather ball
in my hands.
Why I flipped it
hour after hour
into a drooping basket,
until spin and angle
became second nature,
until a perfect rhythm
flooded me.
Shoulders square,
feeling the space
between here and there
down into my toes,
fingers reaching
again and again
for the sky.
Until I gained
a vegetable strength,
inventing the circumstance
of victory,
fat with youth
and youthful delusion,
dancing like a toad
in the reins of fantasy.

FINGERPAINTING

Everybody knows the guy.
The one who sits pouting
in the back of the classroom
with striped pants & greasy hair,
melting crayons on the radiator.
He is the one you dared to eat worms.
The one in high school
who still rode the bus.

He was a slow student,
practiced his one for years
while the others went on
to twos and threes.
He practiced hard,
held his one up late at night
like a bayonet whose warped music
was bent against a stone.

Then one day
he held it straight
and ran all the way to school.
He drew it on the table
to show it
to his teacher
and the table split in two.

DOPPELGANGER

What is at my back
I cannot say,
though I have tried
in any number of subtle ways
to alert someone close to me
into observing it for themselves.
I am beginning to believe
no one else can see it.

The nets are giving way.
Two voices rebound
in the bottom of a grotto,
tangled in orbit, I myself
tangled in this fine grotesque.
In this season of hate,
God is always changing.

We fling the petals
of our life against the wall.
We believe our condition
is permanent & being thus,
easily forgotten.
I pass myself on the road
and try to smile,
but my eyes drop away
full of bees & my teeth
stiffen like hooks.

The golden honey of invisible peace
quivers within me,
but I am so empty
my hunger shames everyone I meet.
The stones roar in greeting
and I grunt hello like a surgeon,
my cages bouncing,
my deepest secret fear
gleaming like a harmony ball.
God is always changing.

When is a man truly free?
Inside or outside himself,
outside a lover
or inside, trembling?
All my opposites are rising now
& clash with my lurid revivability.
I crawl across the dark edge
of the crying Atlantic and peek down.

She crashes at my back door,
leaping like the boy
who sensed he could fly,
who blasted into
the breast of an eagle
and was lost.
God is always changing.

How much brighter
is a dying star?
What fire is spread
by that last breath?
I shiver like a torn curtain,
dreading the last idea,
like a blossom
blown from the dogwood,
dying by itself in the corn.

I stare into the poverty
of the mirror,
where an army of strangers
is continually disfigured,
whispered out of solid water,
each eye leaping from the other,
a mythology of flesh,
birth giving birth giving birth,
death birthing death birthing death.

The first idea was not
our own and we will not
be handed the last.
If we survive,
we win the last decision
by default, seize it,
strangling in seizures,
hands flying out of a form
being riddled with hands,

the last act one action
forgotten into motion,
where deep inside
this flaming digitalis,
surrounded by a hunger of words,
God performs his labor of rock
and is still, **changing** listening **changing.**

THE PLASMA ALLIANCE

Desperate dogs-in-training
roam these streets disguised as men,
homeless and haunted,
dreaming that hard disc accountants
will serve as valets
in the halls of the Plasma Alliance.

They are products
corrupted by the power surge,
a neon blink of history
cooling in silent test tubes.
The men roll up their sleeves
and bare their arms.

Redemption comes quick
as a puncture,
draining the blood
and they're gone,
a cold pint in their pocket,
warm soup in a can.

A woman spanks her child
for staring in disgust
at this poor man.
He stands and motions helplessly
like a painter
who has lost his hands.

THE LAST CANDLE

The mind, by itself, is cold as the surf
and cannot rest. Even in dreams,
the dark beach shifts and bangs against
the ragged winter of memory.
The high wires that drag electricity
into a hundred thousand homes
droop and wrinkle under the weight
of tonight's brilliant storm.
The wind chimes are stripped
from their porches, the lawn chairs tumble,
the rain gallops unbridled with a bad temper,
streaming under collars, breaking tile.
Ahead I see a porthole of light
tremble from between the church doors,
the only fire for miles.

Inside, ten days before Christmas,
an old janitor shuffles from window
to window snuffing the candles.
His cat coughs, sniffing the thin wisps
of paraffin and trails behind.
Soggy, taut as a drumskin,
I settle like a woolly swan in the back.
He nods and leaves me be as I remember
my best friend's voice in the phone
giving up, betraying ten years of sacrifice.
Slowly as seeds soften in plowed ground,
every fear in him spread its fingers
& his heart slipped from my hands like a fish.

Now he hunches, alcoholic, smothered
in the private domain of sleep forever,
like a raccoon staring down the headlights
of a car that never comes.
His body is puffed like an old couch
and legions of women lay their stories
at his feet, his pulse confusing itself
in the dozens of touches like scissors flying.
Time makes a meal of slender talent,
for the germ of an idea that builds
a lonely adoration. For every temple
that makes a music, pretenders climb
rung by rung like psalms, curl into
the mute bell of poverty and wait.

Outside the moths bang madly on the window
like a cloud of lint, anxious
to get at the tiny flame inside,
the last candle of Christmas.
The river lights spill from the gentle hills
dangerously close, glowing with a tragic aura.
Determined shadows climb out
of their manholes and roll East.
At the front of the church two priests emerge
and bicker about luck, the short end
and the long shot, waiting for the janitor
to chase me back into the storm
and finish his chores.
His little gray cat, sticky with wax,
hangs at the altar out of breath.

On the roof, in the wind,
the marble body of Christ
cracks like a wishbone above our heads.

JUNKY

The tracks in your arm
have magisterial access,
a uniform beauty
desperate to belong.
A tourist's enthusiasm takes hold,
pulling your veins
to the surface,
separate trails
leading to a city
you have never known.
You step in.
Invisibly, the citizens feel you up,
welcome you with sticky kisses.
Everywhere the needle lands
feels like the perfect place to go.

THE FOURTH OF JULY

Evil is everybody's business, or lacking that,
everybody's business is evil these days.
The preface of sand is the being that hunts
down mystery or its evil equivalent,
busies itself with innuendo and footprints,
follows the Nile to its conclusion
and traces the two legged outline
whose shadow feet were remembered by mud.
The squid that is the mind,
poisons and conceals, forages and repels
the laws of order.
Whenever the conundrum of loss squeals sharply,
or squirts through the window,
the sand is consulted and falls
piece by piece through the mouth
of the gyre that swallows its own tail
and reveals the spreading tentacles
of the spool unwound,
the threadbare hulk of time tracking itself,
having done what was possible
without mastering the possibilities,
and now, being mastered impossibly
by feathers and fireworks,
tonight, in the sky,
the stone that was our nation
explodes into a thousand probabilities
and measures itself against heaven.

BABY BLAKE

It would have been great
to be the first man,
just think, no potty training
no kindergarten, no trumpet lessons.
No one to tell you what to do.

Just paradise.
Yours to name.
Yours to lose.

When God floated by
like a giant zeppelin
and peered in the window,
the four year old boy
ran screaming to his bedroom,

the same boy who saw
and painted the ghost
of a flea upon his finger,

who saw what carpentry
issues forth
the cornice of the skulls
that the skyscraper rests upon.

Who wondered how many souls
were embedded
in the windows of the moon,

and followed that moon
like a huge jack-o'-lantern
out of his house of feathers
to make his own shelter
fit for the mind's flying.

Whose karmic adoration
lured him into the January forest,
to kneel before a tree

filled with raucous winter angels
shivering palsy-stricken
on every branch.

Their metallic wings were ragged,
bent and beaten, falling
like tattered curtains
down their back,
stripping the frosty leaves
when they fluttered,
jerking in the cold.

Below them, dodging shadows,
misery beetled from hole to hole.

There is no other god before me,
the boy decided,
nothing greater than the door
that opens into the ever-widening
mouth of the night.

What more is needed
to combat Kali Yuga,
"the age of destruction"
than the human form divine,
racing from the granite tower
toward a star of pure delight?

THE BOOK OF DELIVERANCE

Afflicted with a Zen rhetoric,
men die in the privacy of their rooms,
not from a lack of love received,
but from an inability to return it.
Death leaves tributes where it can,
swimming in the center
of the woods at night,
tirelessly holding up the sky.
Below our nature,
a hundred laughing natures lie,
patiently aging in the kingdom of instinct,
waiting for a sudden seizure of conscience,
as God turns in his hiding place,
silently stewing,
like smoke trapped brooding in a glass.
The property of the mind is frail,
filled with wreckage and unmarked trails,
more vows than we can ever remember.
The first page in the book
of deliverance reads **surrender.**

THE SWIMMER

The woman in the pool beside me
tries to catch her breath,
arms whirling like a mill,
hacking at the water
like a beginning sculptor
whose vision outleaps her skill.

What gives way is incidental,
pushing through the path
of least resistance.
Like a sandwich stain
on the corner of an easel,
the ripples from her struggle
are interpreted consciously
and with malice,
accidental though they be.

But the woman, like an artist,
is oblivious, more sure than me.
Smiles leap all over her face
with no place to hide.
New eyes open,
the first of many times.

THE TINY HANDS OF MORNING

In the salty vault of our bodies,
God creeps near, opening and closing
like a rose, a reminder
that if we perfect this life
we will be fitted for another,
fitted together, even if we fall alone,
failing like flakes of snow,
convinced we are the only one of our kind.

The great lights of thunder
beat their saxophone time,
rattling the trees like tambourines.
What we leave will grow,
pushing past the last houses
and the dirty light,
tracing the lines of the river
as it slithers night after night
in the same trail, always suspicious.

The gates of your legs,
with a streaming grace,
open out, and we curl like otters
toward the country we have forgotten,
to the place where the old people,
foggy with questions, disappear
from the edge of the lake.

Look at them.
In these days when survival
depends upon daring,
when beauty is drained by realists
pushing the hive ahead of the bee,
we are alive and awake,
rising and falling side by side
like piano keys.

We are partners in a common darkness,
stitched to the earth
with humble precision,
like the muscles that propel
the mystic energy of the lynx.
The phantoms of morning
have the tiniest hands,
but they are insistent,
so we rise and follow,
groggy with belief.

NERO'S CIRCUS

We might die because we have said so,
walked from the Black Forest,
bald trees in a circle staring,
and blurted a name unthinking
into that startled sky.
Denial ricochets slowly out & back
like a boomerang, bending a little
the will to fly.

Like sharks moving on and on
through black water, they never sleep,
feeding at the edge of night.
Past & Future listen like children.
Desire & Regret dance in their Siamese dress.
Their parents, Knowledge & Oblivion,
stare severely from the silver doorway.

The Red Knight, riding toward the sherbet sun,
steadies his lance, dragons and penguins
and Indians and every kind
of pterodactyl goblin follow him,
seizing their opportunities,
pulling the red from inside the blue,
the blue that lingers in the green.

At some risk, rapture invites itself.
Dazzling apples ripen. The filaments
of the lily shiver with heat.
Supreme exiles sing together
their rhapsodies of departure,
hiding their faces in summer's sad aquarium,
their weary eyes speckled with a strange frost.

The moment you stop looking you will see,
the myth that props the golden boy
on his poster, guilt bursting forth,
when guitars are ashamed to speak
and the opal gleaming in the ape's ascot
becomes an olive in Caesar's teeth.
Violins will arise from the jaws of lions,
out of their maritime prisons,
tearing a freakish song from their strings.

We might die because we have said so,
trundled the past like a baby Pharaoh
and slipped it into a stream.
Many-swaddled lives grip tight
and bump forward, undiscovered,
each shell spinning bankrupt,
pleading with the others to remember
the mercy of the sea.

When music is forced by forgiveness
to howl ambitious beginnings,
the apparitions will mutter of martyrs
prowling past their windows,
fires that won't stay glued to the stake.
They will recall when all beings
belonged equally to the government of water,
its long fingers shining everywhere,
disguised as God.

THE WELL

The well, exhausted, gives up nothing,
has no new secrets, like the mystery
of a woman's mouth that you bite and pull and tug
and suck thinking you might get full,
full as a yellow bee smeared with pollen,
more thirsty as it goes, more desperate.
In over my head, I dig deeper,
drawn by one corner that stays moist
where the sun can't reach.
The mud there is chocolate,
darker than the classic black edge of my shovel
that I hammer into the rib cage of this sneaky pit.
I probe for a wet vein,
an endless distance that might pour in
and swallow me, fill this sad cavity
with a pure tear clear enough to drink.
Late afternoon, my muscles are sick,
surprised by the depth, a sense of falling
into no bottom, surrounded by a silo of stars,
helpless against the spasms of gravity.
Last night my wife dreamed I was a lobster
and she was beneath me,
her hands pinned between my claws,
my legs scratching open her thighs,
the weight of the water pulling us down
into a red blurry cloud of hair.
She fell relenting and awoke to chastise me,
surrounded on all sides by darkness, by water,
by all the things we had taken for granted
and purchased with a pact of silence.
The huge clock threw up its hands in disbelief
while I kissed her honeysuckle fingers back to sleep
and lay there alone in the grim gray light,
searching the clock's moon-white face for a clue.
What rises must live with what descends.
The old standards, the ambiguous impulse,
the worms squirming in the deathbed of my shovel,
the high sweet call of a bird I cannot see
leaking down around me in this hole.

The sky inches by overhead, measuring the earth,
the way the preacher measured me,
just eight years old, knee-deep in salvation,
and he dunked me under once for the Father,
once for the Son, and once for the Holiest Ghost,
each time underwater a kind of death.
I stand as tall as I can, my feet cool and wet,
I reach out and plunge my fist into the black mud.
Eight feet down, an artery of water reaches up.
Trembling like a timid actress in her first premiere,
I wrap the curtain of darkness around me.
I squeeze the handle of my shovel like a snake
and shake my hair like a shroud.
Old blood ticks in the temples of my body
and I breathe deep and I do not answer
and I will not drown.

WHATEVER WEARS THE MASK

We electrocuted Ted Bundy
in Florida today.
Before he shook, he cried once,
and we were asked to beware
the pornographers among us.
The eyes gave no evidence
that J. Edgar Hoover
ever made love with anything.
Dozens of kids in T-shirts
cheered as the hearse passed.
A neon message on a local diner
read Bundy Burn In Hell Special.

If any man ever deserved to die,
it was him, but guilt is magical,
sings us to sleep,
dreaming we are innocent.
Whatever lifts the dark,
or turns the letters,
or wears the mask,
pollutes the sex,
teaches the school,
and dreams the police,
even in the next millennium,
even Year One.

This book was produced using
QuarkXPress on a Macintosh.
The body typestyle is Century Old Style;
titles are set in Folio Bold Condensed.